SOME CLASSIC RULES OF CRICKET

SOME CLASSIC RULES OF
CRICKET

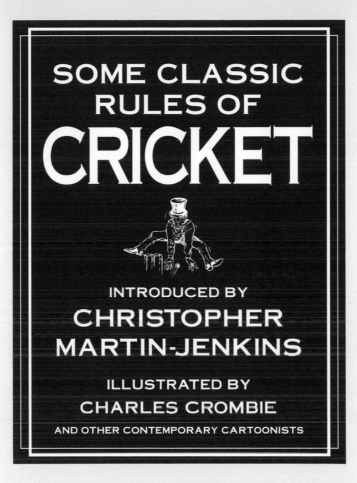

INTRODUCED BY
CHRISTOPHER MARTIN-JENKINS

ILLUSTRATED BY
CHARLES CROMBIE
AND OTHER CONTEMPORARY CARTOONISTS

STUDIO
EDITIONS

This edition published 1994 by Studio Editions Ltd.,
Princess House, 5o Eastcastle Street, London W1N 7AP

Design by Stonecastle Graphics Ltd.
Additional illustrations by Paul B. Davies
Compiled by Christine O'Brien

ISBN 1 85891 164 8

Printed and bound in Singapore

LIST OF ILLUSTRATIONS

INTRODUCTION

But transient is the smile of fate:
A little rule, a little sway,
A sunbeam in a winter's day,
Is all the proud and mighty have
Between the cradle and the grave.

John Dyer's somewhat melancholy, but all too true, sentiments, expressed with equal force and truth by Thomas Gray amongst others, are apt for batsmen too. For some the sunbeam never shines once the first ball has been bowled; and for all batsmen in every innings that little rule, that little sway is subject not just to the wiles of bowlers and the smile or frown of fate, but also to the rules themselves. Or rather, the laws. You can tell cricket is more serious than all other sports by the simple fact that it is actually grave heresy to refer to the laws as rules.

When they became "laws" I am not quite sure, although they were honoured with that title when Marylebone Cricket Club (whose president I once heard introduced by a toastmaster as "president of the Metropolitan Cricket Club") adopted the first of its several codes of laws in May 1774. The first extant set of *rules* was compiled on 11 July 1727 for a match between a side raised by one Mr Broderick of Peper-

harrow, near Godalming in west Surrey, and the Duke of Richmond's team. (The current Duke, by the way, is still involved, as President of Sussex - some things, thank God, don't change much.)

Rules were very clearly required from the moment that the game became something more than one shepherd bowling a stone to another with a stick in front of a wicket gate. Twelve years before that match at Peperharrow, indeed, a Derbyshire man named William Waterfall had been convicted of manslaughter for killing an opponent in a cricket match. Betting on cricket was part of the game's *raison d'être* in the late seventeenth and early eighteenth centuries, and this contributed to the aristocratic infatuation with the game which spread as high as the heir to the throne. Alas, Frederick Prince of Wales died in 1751 as a direct result of an abcess caused by a cricket ball.

Such a "gloriously manly game" demanded strong men to administer it. The two umpires for the Peperharrow match were chosen by the game's two

'If any of the gamesters shall speak...on any point of the game, they are to be turned out...'

patrons, and it was agreed that "if any doubt or dispute arises on any of the aforesaid articles, or whatever else is not settled therein, it shall be determined by the Duke of Richmond and Mr Broderick on their honours". The umpires themselves were protected from intimidation (in theory they have been ever since) by the following strict injunction: "If any of the gamesters shall speak or give their opinion on any point of the game, they are to be turned out and voided in the match". Did I suggest that some things have not changed? Two hundred and sixty-four years later, in 1991, the International Cricket Council (I.C.C.) found it necessary to issue a "Code of Conduct" for all international cricketers, which stated *inter alia*:

> *Players and team officials must at all times accept the umpire's decision. Players must not show dissent at the umpire's decision. Players and team officials shall not intimidate, assault or attempt to intimidate or assault an umpire, another player or a spectator.*

At the same time the I.C.C. introduced a referee for the big international matches to administer this code. For the first time the umpires, hitherto, in Teresa McClean's phrase, the "non-playing monarchs of cricket", were no longer the sole arbiters of the laws.

And yet cricket, in essence, is really quite simple, as an unknown foreigner once proved by this entirely comprehensible explanation:

You have two sides - one out in the field, one in. Each man in the side that's in goes out in turn to have his innings, and when he's out he comes in (or out) and the next man goes in until he's out. Then, when all are out, that ends the innings and the side that's out in the field comes in, and the side that's been in goes out and tries to get those coming in, out. Sometimes, of course, you get men who are still in and not out. When both sides have been in and out, including not outs, that ends the game.

So easy, and yet there was never such a game for esoteric debate about the laws, and often heated debate at that. The recent matter of "ball-tampering" is an unfortunate case in point and one which proves, incidentally, that most laws are designed to make sure that the batsman continues to have the whip hand over the poor, long-suffering workers of the game, the bowlers. It is significant that law 5 on the ball (1980 code) contains five paragraphs, as compared to the one succinct little law on the bat, which merely states the limits of its length (not more than 38 inches), width (not more than 4¼ inches) and that it must be made of wood.

Not only does the ball demand more detailed analysis, but the law-makers found it necessary to return to it in the last and most important law of all, number 42, which deals with unfair play. This begins with the bedrock statement that "the captains are responsible at all times for ensuring that play is conducted within the spirit of the game as well as within the laws".

Note 5 states that "no-one shall rub the ball on the ground or use any artificial substance or take any other action to alter the condition of the ball". Pause for hollowish laughter. Up every hill and down every dale in the English countryside on every weekend in summer some bony seam bowler is slipping a finger-nail under the seam to lift it illegally. It is odd, too, how Australian bowlers of recent vintage seem to have required blobs of nice greasy sun-tan cream, even on the cloudiest days. It is to protect their vulnerable noses, of course. The trouble is that noses have to be blown and scratched occasionally, and foreheads tend to perspire during strenuous exercise, which cannot do any harm to the process of keeping one side of the ball shiny and damp. Any chemist caught with a surplus of sun-tan cream could probably, at a pinch, sell it instead as shoe-polish.

When, however, Pakistani bowlers were alleged to have discovered a new way of swinging an old cricket ball (and, within reason, the older the better) by surreptitiously roughing up one side with bottle-tops or finger-nails, they were subjected by one tabloid newspaper to a prolonged campaign of vilification which ended up in the law courts. No-one, I hope, approved of such skullduggery, but to subject the skulldiggers to

'No-one shall rub the ball on the ground…or take any other action to alter the condition of the ball.'

a Holy War seemed just a little bit over the top, given that this was merely a sophisticated variation on an ancient crime.

As long ago as 1925 there was a hullaballoo when a famous player in the Middlesex *v.* Worcestershire match was accused of lifting the seam; and when England were in South Africa in 1948–49 an umpire even objected to Doug Wright, a leg-spinner of exemplary probity, licking his finger between each ball he bowled. The South African authorities were sensitive about the issue at the time, having just issued an injunction against the use of hair-cream as a polishing agent. In 1931 the Australian Board of Control had similarly banned the use of resin to enable spin bowlers to grip the ball more easily, an edict to which the great leg-spinner Arthur Mailey, amongst others, strongly objected. If wicket-keepers, he argued, could have adhesive aids on their gloves in the form of gripping rubber, and batsmen all the protection their equipment gave them in those less sophisticated days, why should not a bowler be allowed to improve his grip, so long as it did not alter the condition of the ball?

Some of the farcical scenes in cricket are those when umpires, obliged to replace a damaged ball with one of "similar condition" find various ways of instantly ageing its replacement, a sort of reverse Grecian 2000 process. When Reg Perks of Worcestershire once accidentally trod on the ball after only seven balls of

A damaged ball must always be replaced with one of 'similar condition'.

the Hampshire innings, he was obliged to bowl an extra-curricular over to Johnny Arnold, tossing up the last one so that it could be whacked to the boundary, before the game could resume in earnest.

In the 1744 laws the umpires were required to mark the new ball so that they could check that no-one changed it during the course of the match. Not until 1798 was it possible for *both* sides to claim a new ball; and not until the Australians, with their rougher outfields and harder pitches, introduced further help for bowlers in 1901, was it possible to change the ball during an innings, in the first instance after the opposition had reached 200 runs.

Spinners, of course, do not like a new ball. I remember on my first trip to India in 1976–77, in the days of the famous spin quartet of Bedi, Chandrasekhar, Prasanna and Venkataraghavan, how Sunil Gavaskar would sometimes come on for a few overs with the new ball to bowl what was really jokey medium-pace rubbish, so that the sheen on the ball could be disposed of as quickly as possible and the subtler artists enabled to grip the ball.

In a way the history of cricket is the story of the eternal battle for supremacy between the batsmen and the bowlers, and whenever the latter get on top for a while their methods are generally viewed with suspicion, or worse. There was the most almighty upheaval in 1980–81 in Australia in a one-day international,

The eternal battle for supremacy between the batsman and bowler.

when the captain Greg Chappell instructed his brother Trevor to bowl what prep-school boys used to call a "sneak" (an underarm grubber) to prevent New Zealand scoring a six off the last ball of the match. This was a clear case of something being within the law but without its spirit.

True to cricket history, the law was promptly changed to bar underarm bowling in limited-overs games. Yet there had been days in which roundarm bowling, let alone overarm, had caused equal horror amongst batsmen. It was unfair, they said, and would ruin the game. I half expected England's batsmen to claim that Shane Warne's leg-breaks were in some way unfair or illegal after he had bowled Mike Gatting with a freakish delivery, the first he had ever bowled in a Test in England, in the opening game of the 1993 rubber at Old Trafford.

Stopping the fast bowlers from threatening batsmen's lives with bouncers has been the greater concern of legislators in the last fifty years; but if Warne keeps bowling sides out and inspires too many successful imitators, you may be sure that someone will want to change the law.

Christopher Martin-Jenkins

He does not know how to handle a bat
Any more than a dog or a cat.

WILLIAM BLAKE, *AN ISLAND IN THE MOON*, 1787

THE BOUNDARY.

When the ball touches a boundary it becomes "Dead". The Umpire is not a boundary.

PLATE 1

Together joined in cricket's manly toil...
All, all that brother should be, but the name.

LORD BYRON, *HOURS OF IDLENESS*, 1807

THE GAME

2. The choice of innings shall be decided by tossing.

PLATE 2

The very names of a cricket bat and ball
make English fingers tingle.

WILLIAM HAZLITT, *THE NEW MONTHLY MAGAZINE*, 1825

PLATE 3

Every ball that he bowled had brain behind it,
if not exactness of pitch.

A. G. MACDONELL, *ENGLAND, THEIR ENGLAND*, 1933

HOW TO PLACE MEN IN THE FIELD.

V.—

To a fast left-handed bowler, a long-leg is seldom necessary.

PLATE 4

See the son of grief at cricket
Trying to be glad.

A. E. HOUSMAN, *A SHROPSHIRE LAD*, 1896

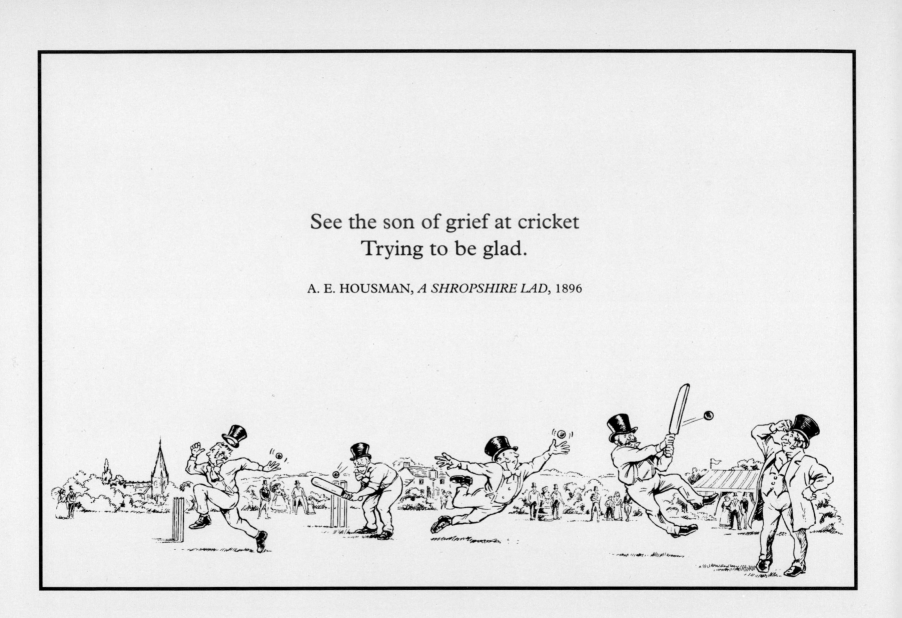

9. The innings shall commence, after the ground has been swept and rolled unless the In-side object.

PLATE 5

But cricket is full of glorious chances, and the goddess who presides over it loves to bring down the most skilful players.

THOMAS HUGHES, *TOM BROWN'S SCHOOL DAYS*, 1857

PLATE 6

In matters of grave importance, style,
not sincerity, is the vital thing.

OSCAR WILDE, *THE IMPORTANCE OF BEING EARNEST*, 1895

13. When (in the opinion of the Umpire) six balls have been bowled he shall call... "Over."

PLATE 7

Boys are capital fellows in their own way, among their mates;
but they are unwholesome companions for grown people.

CHARLES LAMB, *ESSAYS OF ELIA*, 1823

PLATE 8

Each fresh batsman is a fresh beginning to the game.
He comes in unready, a hope to the bowler.

E. F. BENSON AND EUSTACE MILES,
THE CRICKET OF ABEL, HIRST AND SHREWSBURY, 1903

15. The bowler may *make* the batsman (at the end from which he is bowling) stand on any side of the wicket which he may direct.

PLATE 9

Let us be thankful for the fools. But for them
the rest of us could not succeed.

MARK TWAIN, *FOLLOWING THE EQUATOR*, 1897

PLATE 10

Cricket. A sport at which contenders drive a ball
with sticks or bats in opposition to each other.

SAMUEL JOHNSON, *A DICTIONARY OF*
THE ENGLISH LANGUAGE, 1755

"Caught"

22. If the ball, from a stroke of the bat··· be held ·· although·· hugged to the body of the catcher :– The STRIKER is out.

PLATE 11

I never was a boy, never played at cricket;
it is better to let Nature take her course.

JOHN STUART MILL, *AUTOBIOGRAPHY*, 1867

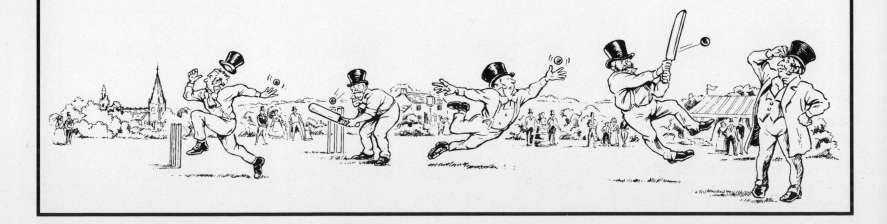

32. The striker being caught, no runs shall be scored.

PLATE 12

Judgement as to how and when to run is one
of the characteristics of a good batsman.

W. G. GRACE, *CRICKET*, 1891

LOST BALL
34. If the ball cannot be found Six runs shall be added.

PLATE 13

'Tis with our judgements as our watches, none
Go just alike, yet each believes his own.

ALEXANDER POPE, *AN ESSAY ON CRITICISM*, 1711

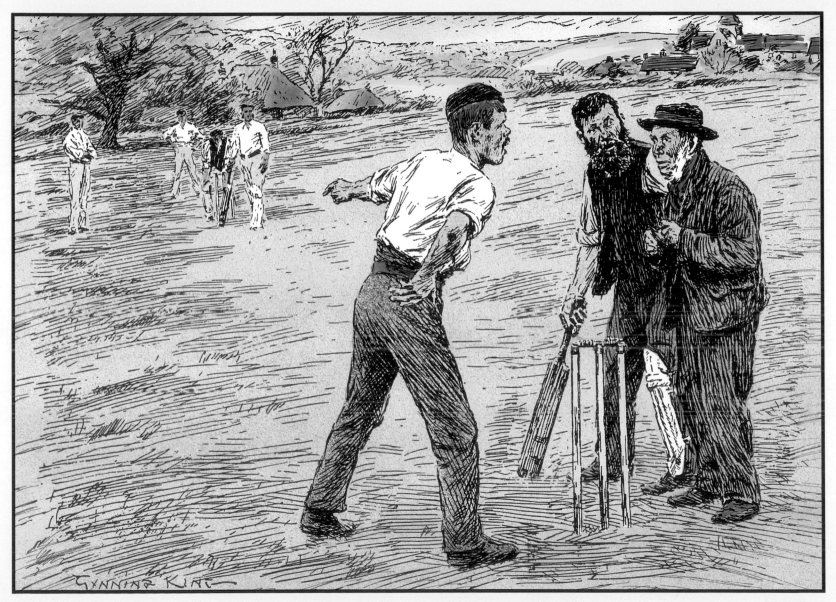

GYNNING KING

PLATE 14

Fielding is the only branch of the game in which,
if one tries hard enough, one can be sure of success.

K. S. RANJITSINHJI, *THE JUBILEE BOOK OF CRICKET*, 1897

"The FIELDSMAN."

41. If he wilfully stop the ball otherwise·· than with his person· five runs shall be·· added to the score.

PLATE 15

Gentleman batters were common:
gentleman bowlers were quite another dish.

GEORGE MEREDITH, *ADVENTURES OF HARRY RICHMOND*, 1871

PLATE 16

What, frighted with false fire?

WILLIAM SHAKESPEARE,
HAMLET, PRINCE OF DENMARK, 1600

WICKET KEEPER.
42 – If the wicket-keeper incommode the striker by any noise or commotion the striker shall not be put out.

PLATE 17

And when a lady's in the case,
You know, all other things give place.

JOHN GAY, *FABLES*, 1712

INSTRUCTIONS TO UMPIRES.
47~48, An umpire should not
allow himself to be unduly
influenced by appeals.
  If he be in any doubt, LAW
43, *"That the existing state
of things shall continue,"*
shall be followed.

PLATE 18